T0394884

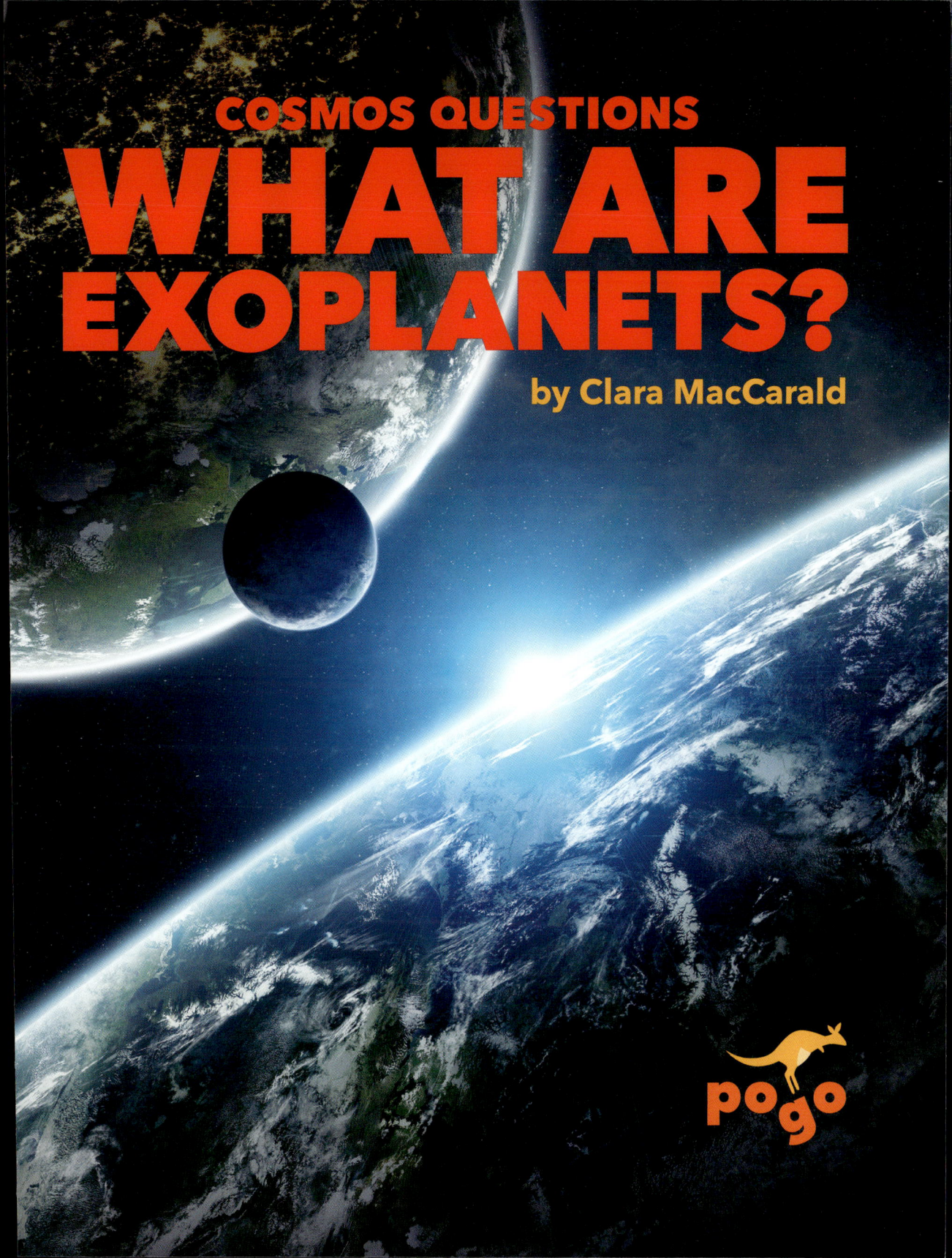

COSMOS QUESTIONS

WHAT ARE EXOPLANETS?

by Clara MacCarald

po**g**o

Ideas for Parents and Teachers

Pogo Books let children practice reading informational text while introducing them to nonfiction features such as headings, labels, sidebars, maps, and diagrams, as well as a table of contents, glossary, and index.

Carefully leveled text with a strong photo match offers early fluent readers the support they need to succeed.

Before Reading

- "Walk" through the book and point out the various nonfiction features. Ask the student what purpose each feature serves.
- Look at the glossary together. Read and discuss the words.

During Reading

- Have the child read the book independently.
- Invite them to list questions that arise from reading.

After Reading

- Discuss the child's questions. Talk about how they might find answers to those questions.
- Prompt the child to think more. Ask: Do you think scientists will find life on exoplanets? Why or why not?

Pogo Books are published by Jump!
5357 Penn Avenue South
Minneapolis, MN 55419
www.jumplibrary.com

Jump! is a division of FlutterBee Education Group.

Library of Congress Cataloging-in-Publication Data

Names: MacCarald, Clara, 1979- author.
Title: What are exoplanets? / by Clara MacCarald.
Description: Minneapolis, MN: Jump!, Inc., [2026]
Series: Cosmos questions | Includes index.
Audience: Ages 7-10
Identifiers: LCCN 2024053611 (print)
LCCN 2024053612 (ebook)
ISBN 9798892138581 (hardcover)
ISBN 9798892138598 (paperback)
ISBN 9798892138604 (ebook)
Subjects: LCSH: Extrasolar planets–Juvenile literature.
Classification: LCC QB820 .M38 2026 (print)
LCC QB820 (ebook)
DDC 523.2/4–dc23/eng/20241226
LC record available at https://lccn.loc.gov/2024053611
LC ebook record available at https://lccn.loc.gov/2024053612

Editor: Alyssa Sorenson
Designer: Emma Almgren-Bersie

Photo Credits: JPL-Caltech/NASA, cover; sdecoret/Adobe Stock, 1; Dotted Yeti/Shutterstock, 3, 8; Alex Mit/Adobe Stock, 4; Sergey Nivens/Adobe Stock, 5; Sunflower/Adobe Stock, 6-7; amriphoto/iStock, 9; RON MILLER/Science Source, 10-11; Manuel Mata/Adobe Stock, 11; Skórzewiak/Adobe Stock, 12-13; 3000ad/Adobe Stock, 14-15; remotevfx/Shutterstock, 16; MARK GARLICK/Science Source, 17; janez volmajer/Adobe Stock, 18-19; dottedyeti/Adobe Stock, 20-21; alejomiranda/iStock, 23.

Printed in the United States of America at Corporate Graphics in North Mankato, Minnesota.

TABLE OF CONTENTS

CHAPTER 1

PLANETS

Milky Way

The **universe** holds everything that exists. This includes outer space, stars, planets, and you! The universe has billions of **galaxies**, too. We live in the Milky Way galaxy.

Billions of stars are in our galaxy. The Sun is one of them. It is the center of our **solar system**. Planets and other space objects **orbit** the Sun.

Sun

Our solar system has eight planets. Mercury, Venus, Earth, and Mars are closest to the Sun. They are rocky. They have surfaces to stand on. Earth is the only planet we know that has life.

The four planets farther from the Sun do not have hard surfaces. Jupiter and Saturn are mostly made of gases. They are gas giants. Uranus and Neptune have ice and gases. They are ice giants.

DID YOU KNOW?

Earth is in our solar system's **habitable** zone. It is the perfect distance from the Sun for liquid water to exist. Water is needed for life.

MERCURY

SUN

JUPITER

NEPTUNE

URANUS

EARTH

VENUS

SATURN

MARS

CHAPTER 2

EXOPLANETS EVERYWHERE

Our solar system isn't the only one with planets. Planets outside our solar system are called exoplanets.

We know of more than 5,600 exoplanets in the Milky Way. There might be billions more!

The closest exoplanet to Earth is Proxima Centauri b. Scientists think it may be rocky like Earth. It may have water and life! Proxima Centauri b is four **light-years** away. If an airplane could fly there, the trip would take 5 million years!

Proxima Centauri b

Exoplanets are everywhere. Each star may have at least one exoplanet orbiting it. Some orbit their star quickly. A year may only be a few days long. Some orbit two stars instead of one.

Rogue exoplanets wander the universe alone. Why? They may have been pushed out of a star's orbit. Or they may have formed in the middle of nowhere.

Like the planets in our solar system, some exoplanets are rocky. Others are made of gas. They are different sizes, too. Some have strange weather. One has rainstorms of glass. Another rains melted iron. Some have oceans of lava!

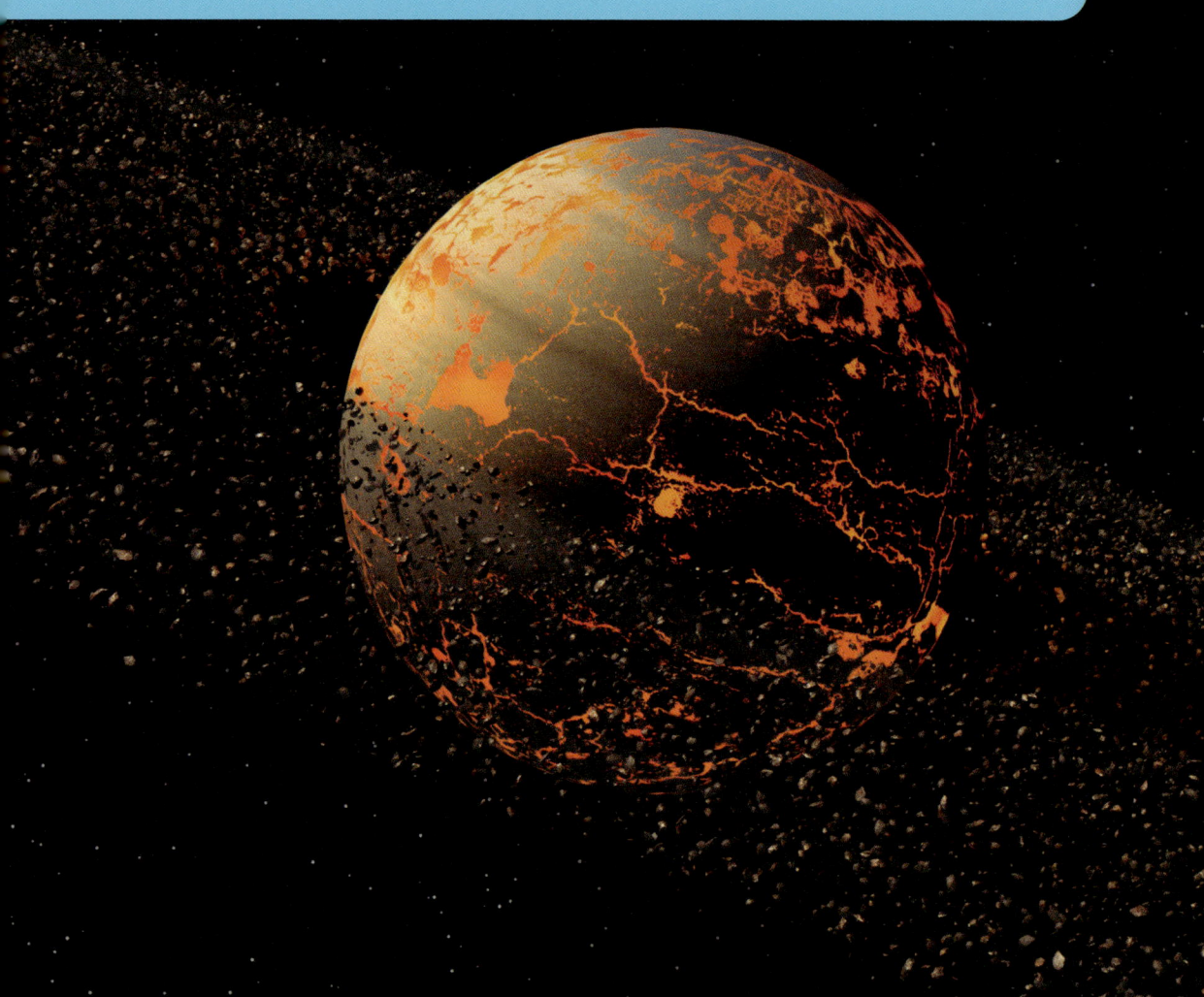

TAKE A LOOK!

Scientists have grouped exoplanets into four types.
Take a look!

GAS GIANT

- as large or larger than Jupiter or Saturn
- made mostly of gas

NEPTUNIAN

- about the same size as Uranus and Neptune
- made mostly of gas

SUPER-EARTH

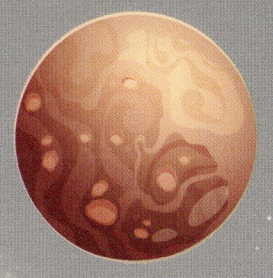

- smaller than Neptune and larger than Earth
- made of rock, gas, or both

TERRESTRIAL

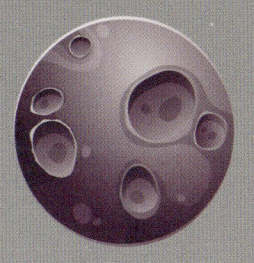

- the same size as Earth or smaller
- made of metal and rock

CHAPTER 3

FINDING EXOPLANETS

Exoplanets are hard to find. Why? They are many light-years away.

Satellites help. They record the sky. Scientists look closely at the **data**. They search for signs of exoplanets.

satellite

Scientists look for stars that get dim and bright again. Why? There could be an exoplanet blocking the star's light as it moves past.

Scientists also watch how stars move. A star's **gravity** pulls on exoplanets. Exoplanets pull back. This causes the star to sway a little.

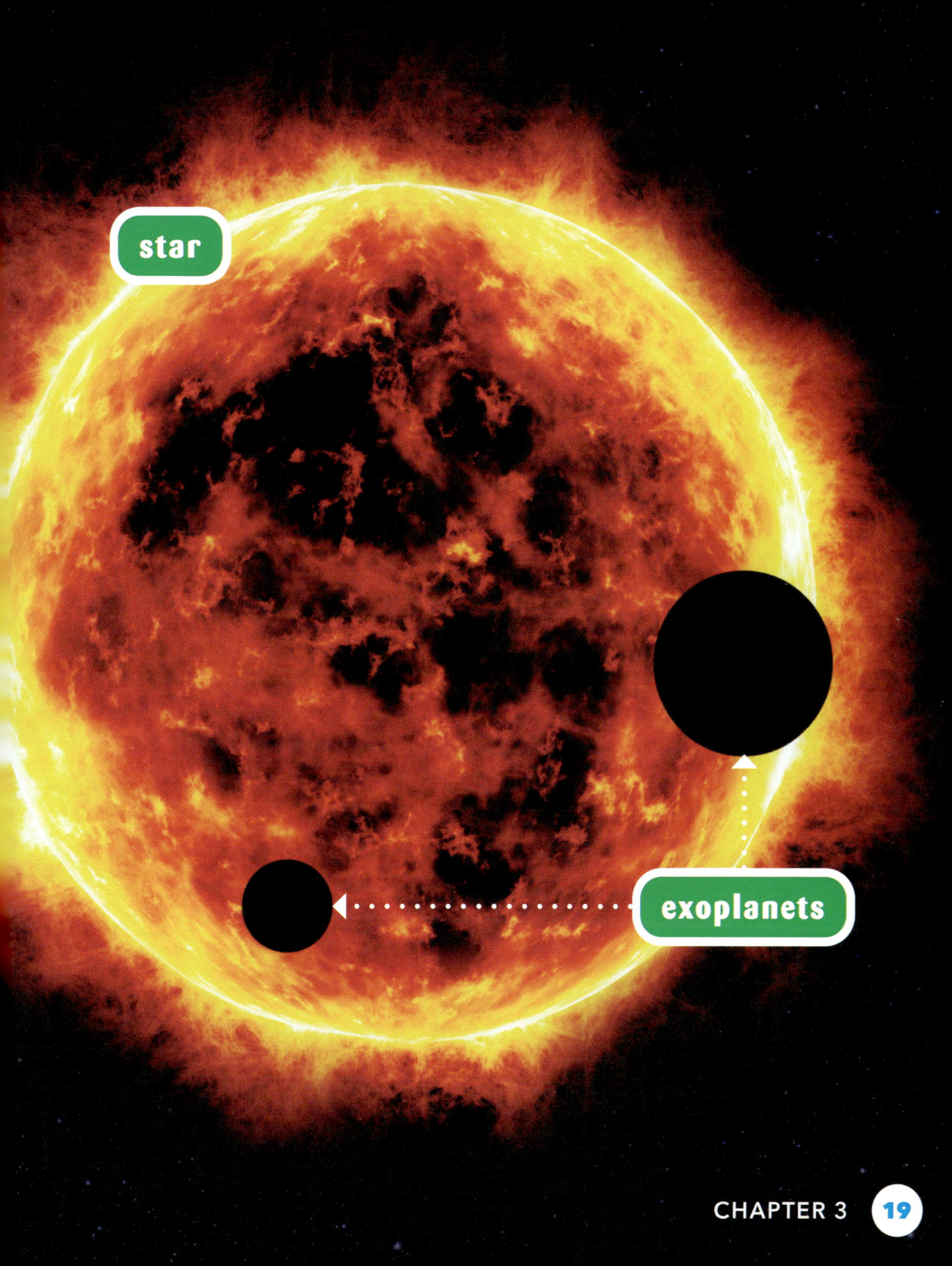

star

exoplanets

Is there life on exoplanets? Scientists are looking! They search for rocky exoplanets. These exoplanets need to be in a star's habitable zone. Liquid water might be there. Life as we know it needs water. Scientists also look for exoplanets that have an **atmosphere** like Earth. Someday, scientists might find out that we are not alone!

DID YOU KNOW?

TRAPPIST-1 is a star. It is 40 light-years from us. Seven rocky exoplanets orbit it. Three might have liquid water!

ACTIVITIES & TOOLS

BLOCKING A STAR

How does an exoplanet block a star's light? Find out with this fun activity!

What You Need:
- flashlight
- dark room
- objects of different sizes, such as a pencil, eraser, tennis ball, and hairbrush

1. **Go into a dark room. Turn on your flashlight. Shine it on the wall. The light is your star.**

2. **Hold a pencil between the light and wall. The pencil is your exoplanet. What happens to the light when you do this?**

3. **Move the pencil closer to the light. Move it farther away. What happens to the light?**

4. **Try other objects in front of the light. What happens when the object is bigger? What about when it is smaller?**

5. **How do your findings connect to scientists looking for exoplanets?**

GLOSSARY

atmosphere: The mixture of gases that surrounds a planet.

data: Information collected so something can be done with it.

galaxies: Very large groups of stars and planets.

gravity: The force that pulls things toward the center of a space object and keeps them from floating away.

habitable: Safe and good enough to live in.

light-years: Measures of distance in space. One light-year is 5.9 trillion miles (9.5 trillion kilometers).

orbit: To travel in a circular path around something.

rogue: Behaving in a way that is not expected or normal.

satellites: Spacecraft sent into orbit around Earth, the Moon, or another space object.

solar system: The Sun, together with its orbiting bodies, as well as asteroids, comets, and meteors.

universe: All existing matter and space.

INDEX

TO LEARN MORE

Finding more information is as easy as 1, 2, 3.

❶ Go to www.factsurfer.com

❷ Enter "exoplanets" into the search box.

❸ Choose your book to see a list of websites.

FACT SURFER